Azure Blues

AZURE BLUES

Gerry Gilbert

Talonbooks   •   Vancouver   •   1991

published with the assistance of The Canada Council

Talonbooks
201 / 1019 East Cordova Street
Vancouver
British Columbia, V6A 1M6
Canada

Typeset in Caslon 540, Futura Medium and Futura Demi, by Pièce de Résistance Ltée. and printed and bound in Canada by Hignell Printing Ltd.

First printing: January 1991

Many of these poems first appeared: for the readers of *Attitude, Berkeley Horse, Capilano Review, Downtown Eastside Poetry Project, From Next Spring, Front, Ganglia, Georgia Straight, Radio Waves, Vancouver Review, Vancouver Sun, White Lunch,* and *Zajets*; for audiences at the Dance Centre's production "City on the Edge," and Edam's production, "Critical Mass," and at poetry readings in Vancouver, Victoria, Calgary, Edmonton, Saskatoon, Regina, Winnipeg, Toronto, Ottawa, and on Denman Island; and for listeners to "In Other Words," "Fine Lines," "Prismatic," and "Radiofreerainforest" on radio and to the audiotape "The Invention of Language," recorded with the Paul Plimley Trio.

Canadian Cataloguing in Publication Data

Gilbert, Gerry, 1936–
  Azure Blues

Poems.
ISBN 0-88922-286-X

I. Title.
PS8563.I47A9 1990   C811'.54   C90-091759-8
PR9199.3.G54A9 1990

CONTENTS

PRETEXT

I started '86's writing the previous November and when the year of the rush appeared I was on duty and I was still up there when it went the way of all numbers and in February '87, three months ago, I let go. It's the night of the day now.

This isn't writing. This is washing out the frying pan, the cocoa-ing cup, the chewing cap.

I dropped everything in March and called a concert and annual reported a cool ninety minutes.

This has got to be the wrong way to put it. Why do I persist? I just started smoking again. I quit in April, six weeks ago Monday. My arm is better but not for throwing. The stitches have healed but the skin around the eye there still feels thin. Wednesday, the bicycle dropped me. My right arm learned to use chop sticks. I don't have in mind any particular literary way of moving this preamble. I persisted in thinking that that limp into my fifty-second year was some kind of a beginning, so I let there be no more coffee or money or intoxication or clean laundry or language in the house. I finished what I was reading. I vacuumed. I forgot to set the clock ahead. I didn't get the grant. I didn't do my income tax. I gave up on history and common sense gave up all over me.

The rest is verse.

Fork

stick around
or
the poem may never end

HOW TO EAT A PEACH

Pray Tell

when you can't think of anything
turn a page

when you laugh
everywhere you look laughs
that's the 2 of you

when you come to a word
it's only so that
the word can come to you

it's rush hour
i'm thinking to myself:
don't think of anything but what you are doing!

but what i'm doing is coming to see you

when you can't think of everything
close the book

From the Tune of "Fools Rush In"

"you're an authoritarian"
you said
& i agreed
we are all of us authors
some of us are aries

are those 2 ashtrays
or am i 2 eyes
what does the nose know

pinch that roach
pump that pedal
write that down

no skunk cabbage
not much of a swamp

Dark Years Apart

we flattened the grass
but that was last night
i get fat just thinking about it
i crawled around your clothes
you climbed through mine
the light we were fell down over there
only to rise up again right here

is that a slug or a map of california
is it right or is it writing
is it wrong or is it song

full size is very small
like looks
we send out
for everything to happen to

Absotively Posilute

think of a place you can't smoke
you can't even wear your shoes
slugs are rolling pellets of catfood around the floor
the party only the dancers survived
there's no tv so you watch the door
just standing beside a bicycle is enough to knock you over on your knee
like a government's idea of who you might be
but tomorrow is all you're ready for

think of all the spots of power you fell over
learning to write finer than you can read
better to sleep on both pillows yourself
than to awaken tail first every day
meaning it there but not meaning it here
dreaming of being addicted to privacy

Dream

i tossed the automatic under the pillow
but is it art
the pistol under the other pillow is real enough

i go out & leave you there behind the piano
but the guard locks the door behind me
i should tell him there's someone left behind

when the rational is seen as a machinery
as a threat to the organic
try eating vietnamese style crab
uncracked in spicy garlic sauce
at half price
with only your teeth & fingers
without thinking about it
& eventually figuring it out

Bursts of Friendliness

when a chunk of the story repeats itself
& homer & chandler do it all the time
there's a faintly mental smell
& you can tell
you're in the presence of poetry

i went to the convention of
the american institute for the conservation of
historic & artistic works
saying
i heard there was someone here
who could make my poems last forever

rock & roll is all one song
kids want to be beautiful
any poem is one more

Sight Buds

look out
they're looking out

worm-wet monday afternoon
human creature viewing splendour

hasti
hastings

this mind is too small for both of us
that's not what he wished were so

around here only dirty dishes amount to anything
why are those flies hanging around the typewriter

the grass so high this summer
i only know when i'm not

that's enough of me
for this citee

Walking There

don't make big decisions in the summer
the facts don't weigh very much
ontario's having an election
the u.s. navy's in vancouver
& everyone else you see realizes
we're on our own here
defeated on a bench in victory square
watching the movie crews
& the tramps flow through
what's the matter?
bird got your crumb?
the hum of the traffic
the skin of the drum
new news & old shoes

Make Your Point & Move On

chewing gum
smoking tobacco
cracking sunflower seed
talking tongue

august tomorrow
there was still snow on the mountains 2 or 3 weeks ago
north shorn

easy picking for the herring
easy pickin' for the heron

think again
i said to the caterpillar

the cemetery is how
all summer they don't allow
artificial flowers

Canada's a Nice Place to Read but I Wouldn't Wanna Write There

one loves
the feeding
of another's hunger
so much
it makes me understand
just why
the poor
are always with us
we
who are
at once
so unjust
& so
generous

Idle Idol Idyl

a good movie will kick you out for months
weeks life

won't wait
too late

a landscape
to boot

the weeds
are agreed

just another year
out here

once & for all
the world

rather an acrobat
than an actor be

Easy Reader

the extractor
at the laundry
wasn't working
but i managed
to say

if i'd
a known
i wouldn't a put
a quarter
in it

rather than argue
with the attendant
who knows enough
not to admit it

Defective Story

if i think about it
i got nothing to do
i'm covered
i can sleep if i want to

not watching tv every day
improves your dreams every night

the flies can always get in
but they can't get out if you don't open the window

as for the wasps
catch them with a glass & a postcard from the english dep't

work out similarity
play upon difference
rest in forgetfulness

Less

whatever became of art
somebody tap dancing on an escalator
flicking a cigarette against the black glass window of a passing limo
sleaze at any price an indefinite article of faith

"gotta wonder about people walking along with a smile on their face"
"& in dark pants"
says the next table

trans romantic
mid specific

i forget what i was going today

NANAIMO BOMB

THE COURTYARD

can you hear the restaurant ventilator fan
waiting for the courtyard to fill with conversation

generation
generation

& every plant & animal in the world is food

if i didn't bring the bike in from the alley
i don't have to

imagine what i could say if i wouldn't write

& so we sit
impossible
& so we stand

a faded vancouver style green of late august
the body temperature of peter's sweatshirt
gerry's jacket
woodshed wall of old chinese paint in the doorway
exterior matrix of light & thought

turn on
as we used to say
smoke that hibachi
charcoal & ronsonol
& the faded green of the ferns too
under the ivy
the ivy
never fades
never shaves
becomes fence roof tree
lives on the catshit under the holly
& don't we all
or what's a poem about
eh stan

"slunge"
it said on the hospital door i opened to see
looked like a broomcloset to me
a sink for the entrails maybe

"mind your own business"
slammed the nurse

slunge!

& i raise my words
& wash down the years   .

RESISTANCE
for the 1987 B.C. General Strike

seagull flies
by line of eye to a
crime of desire

"a man who could stand electricity
used his hands' fingers
to test the sockets in our house
said 'you build resistance'
lined us boys up & passed the current through us
for fun
knew electricity really
before there was
much"

the seagull
circles the spot for us
out on the milo river
poet chu yuan
way back when
protesting the corrupt government of his day
let go breath
& leapt in &
we're still racing to the rescue

i write this poem under protest
i could be bringing in the garbage
eating the carpet
melting down the tv
throwing the dirty dishes through the picture window
here at the beginning of the rainbow
where us bad guys live
the good guys live at the end of the rainbow
selfishness itself
we have a misunderstanding with them
we always miss
they always understand
making away with the levelution
getting crafty in their old age
it feels like our imaginations have been logged
b.c. the quietest place in the language
this is what the free world is fighting for
the pacified coast
governed by charlie m¢¢arthy & the forty thieves
is the poem over yet?
i wish i wasn't so bad
but that's like wishing wealth hadn't become money
or compassion hadn't become power
or that our molecules would stop milling about
all this kettle needs is a spout
do i have to spell it out

"will the seagull chase you"

"only if you run
friend
only if you run"

the rabid right
has got all night

bad luck rules
in a land of fools

vander zalm the disaster
a power tool in the hand of what master

social credit's a superstition
the fantasy garden of the inquisition

well what do you know
there's nowhere to go

the creation of day
we open our eyes & stand in the way

this space pecked into a decision
man o man seagull struts away
a little whiter

"this time"
boy o boy seagull cries & cries "this time"
this time

hear
say

a world
away

what
we

lost
asleep

who
me

yes
you

will
awake

hungry
the next seagull you see
saw you first

FILM REVIEW:
Alsino & The Condor (Nicaragua 1982)

rebellion & repression in central america
the view from the village
a who's who of life in the war zone
told by a boy with "the hands of a man/the eyes of a child"
he drapes his pissy bedding over the barbed wire
(we'll hang out our laundry on the . . .)
the innate desire-for-freedom's flow up
like a bird's
from grandmother's hearth to the guerillas' mountains
the only time she knows is when to plant & when to eat
the boy searches through his father's chest for the world
the telescope he finds just makes him lonely
the magic word's a name saying nothing
drops him from the sky & breaks his back
& so he finds the world after all
as aeschylus would say "begin the play in the sorrow of the survivors
   we all are"
there's people shot & burned in the ground & dissolved in the river
there's killers maddened by fear
there's americans crazed by disgust
there's a man of his word, the schoolteacher, dies a poet
there's the village bullshitter sells the truth to save his skin
there's the man who thinks he's free
dislocates the wings of birds for a living
art that puts a cage around life
that makes hope the trick of the impossible promise
there's religion coming true
"find your own cross" says the actor when the kid's just trying to help
"get me down from here!" says the actor when the flames find out it's
   made of wood

there's a circus comes to town every year from the conquistadores
   through the yankees, all those wax wings
murderers with good intentions
but there is no just kind temperate brutality
the sky is for the birds
the ground belongs to the people

MY KNIFE
WANTS A HARLEY

getting away
with reality
again today

Or

at the foot of
well we'll get to that later
what we're at the foot of

back against the seawall
actually back to the bicycle for the paper & pencil
& on to
onto the rock

tide's in
here's the dirt

i don't have eighteen million dollars
but the commonwealth rulers are in town anyway
so there i am at pender & burrard
giving the motorcade the leather finger
on behalf of the common poverty
proud & tall
toothpick in my teeth
the language
& it shows
the spy in the deathseat of the lead carcar thinks so
i see him spot me & i don't compute
i'm supposed to be wet
but i'm burning

forget the sunset
man
i'm the view

kinda makes your feet sweat
doesn't it
don't slip

You're Listening to Vancouver Co-op Radio
(B.C.'s National Magazine)

settle in to the best seat in the theatre
a bare inch from the gentle lips kissing your mind
the clean teeth chewing your dreams

lean over the leading edge of b.c. imagery
your listening creates these poems
as truly as the writing gives them voice

there's ghosts in them there words

yes but
is is is
rain rain rain
radiofreerainforest

sunday night at nine
alternate thursdays at four-thirty

cfr-
co-op radi-
oh-oh

Artropolis

i see
the art
you see

we stop for nickles

octogre
an act of sunshine
one day bemused
amazed another

dad dancing to the fine old sound of the water heater crumbling

this essay i'm thinking about that i read today
if not this sentence itself
proceeds by thinking for you if you're not careful
cleverly alienating you with its usefulness
from the subject
subject indeed
objects that bleed
a usefulness that appropriates what's being talked about
privatising it
using it as proof of some hairnet belief that you'll buy

you falls upon you bed
you skinny hands around you bony head

SINGS
CONDITION

Winter Taming

stroke the furnace
love jealousy
purvey fine memory since one million bc
goose the lazy rooster
wait for saturday even if it takes until next thursday
hide range rustle
bare leaf reason

it's dead but it looks good
make it a product
give it a price
take it away from those who need it most
want it best
get it last
hope falls eternal

Town of Vice

i know what i'm not doing
you can't start me now

sure, it was a mistake
like summer ending on labour day

putting a comma there
a comment here

god i loved you
that was us

medicine is hearsay
would that there were no good reasons for what i say

surprising silence
a taste of fresh water

just sneaking peeks
only magnifies the city

With it Without

the panic i felt when i saw i was going to have to sit through that
some of that
again

i guess it's good enough for writing to
is this the theatre of canada
what don't you know

everything says
nothing we say
ever said so

i.e. dance comix
like it only hurts when you read up the edge
of the page

language knows
yes you

Talk = Action & Zero

kakania as "the utopia of the status quo" (R. Musil)
"adanac is the vessel of the eternal present . . . no peculiarities,
    only tics . . ." (P. Culley)

RECOVERY BEGINS AFTER FIRES

the phone could ring
i could have eaten those sardines
where could paws have gone with my last quarter
i could become a skilled electrician

the coffee of the year maybe but not this one
what he knows runneth over
don't you ever talk about me in the third person she said
this can be written

the mail order houses get the clever calculators first
concentration in the form of a species
who put the spin in mrs murphy's gin
my life is what the universe expands into

a garbage truck rising through the gears drives by
3 times i had to leave early in homage
i started as a part-time volunteer in damage control
controversy jerks along

you are so tight because you fit so well together
i forget until i don't have to remember
there goes an unequivocal carbon copy
i get my thrills bulk erasing tapes

there's no music for this
i can feel the way i can't help
having heard nothing i said everything having heard everything i said this
so what makes good shirts

sides don't have things things have sides
some nights you stay up for
nothing stops at a cup of coffee & the kettle's on
i sit accused to the chair voting on my but as i dislike

would you like to hear my hurricane gilbert headlines or
my arguments for steve mccaffery
i refuse to quote peanuts anymore than i have to it's not me it's my runners
the theory of drinking is not very good at predicting the theory of smoking

1 pkg of imperialism & 3 revolutions please
the mouse trap game doesn't work any more
hair hangs on
work the radio play yourself wax the moons of your boots

NOVEMBER

forget art
if it's just another song for the u.s. market
or who's?
to lose

free trade
lose the country
nuclear subs
lose the world

the mock in democracy
the pain in campaign
calling all canadians
fall apart again

can odd breadbent
& glass jaw turnip
upstooge
barn not brains baloony?

yope
nup
think of a century
slowing up

a b.c. dog & a washington dog meet at the border
"how come you're so skinny" says the washington dog
"how come you can't bark" says the b.c. dog
the free trade deal is a canada-wide out on the country

feeling chilly?
cuba nicaragua
the canadas
the ends of the americas

"canadian justice stinks"
said leonard peltier when we gave him back to the f.b.i.
perhaps we should have canadian content rules in the legal system
canadian contentment rules in the bookstores

to get back into power
the liberals & conservatives let their loss leaders say anything they want
canada should clear its throat
too bad the n.d.p. can't afford your vote

openness
restructuring
the whistling in the window
i don't know about me & that goes for you too

this has been a refried urpolitical nonsensement
brought to you by the rent party
which will keep you deformed
as invents unshrivel

PRONOUNS WILD
for bp

Plug

it's not the thing
it's the thought
things being
the way thoughts are

so think of a thing
that won't happen
no matter what you think
& there you are

the way
down which what can't happen
just might
as well be you

in
the way

•

sinners are their own best enemies
winners are their own worst friends

●

strides
we called our black denim jeans
draped
pegged
9 buttons high
school in 1952
if you hadn't ever accidently cut into yourself with your own shiv for
    a look you were fresh out
we called dinks tools
& jacked off by pure thought
stung vets of bb pistol battle games in the bushes beyond civilization
the shield shaped ww 2 service badges in our dads' noncom lapels
    already tarnishing
i never wanted to be an officer
i'd take the icecream cone away from any kid who believed in it
ever the joker in the gang
always offering something amazing to say
we don't own the mountain it owns us
drunk out of our skulls on grouse
or in the balcony of the avon theatre watching shakespeare on stage writing
down the stairs into the golden lobby bobbing in our life lit teentime eyes
the steps under our feet a cadenza by les paul
intermission arguments in lines from l'étranger
& out on hastings the streetlamps in the black rain shone like a brass band
there to light the people

the chinese tailor in the unit block west pender who made those bad
    pants for all the good hoods
has closed up shop as of this summer 35 years later
crates we called our bicycles
boys
west side white
not a head line in sight
sniffing at history
i made a few bucks at a craps stag one afternoon late in grade 12
& never went back
a lot of those guys still live there
right away i moved downtown
& pretty soon here up the inlet to side city
this must be our next conversation
we never met a boys' club we couldn't elude
we give listen

•

"a postcard from vancouver"
i mime to you
& strike a brave pose on my new 12 speed balloon-tired black & silver
    narrative device
you don't quite catch my drift
& shrug
"yeah?"
& climb painfully into the car
& i see the fix you are in
& i'm ashamed for flaunting my agility
by '65 we'd already met on paper
paid lavish attention to each other's work ever since

& we'd see each other over the fancy & hug hands on it
"i've got nothing to say & i'm saying it"
the first language you ever need
i sit here listening to the rain
watching the o's on the page spin grip & roll
growing up up & away

•

sc
ratch!
the nib
new
suck the wax off

beepbeepbeepbeep
hop to the desk & flip the tape to the other side of the other side of
    dexter gordon

like
the disinterest rate the cold world has for the warm
arm
hard to get my hunger to make all gold worthless in the mood these days
but there's a lot of hay needs making down on the slang farm
it's going to be a long old winter doing what we're told

i hear on the radio that gun control is banned in the bible
i suppose it is the same old poem
it certainly is the same old story

sitting in the movie
eyes wide open
waiting until all the facts are in

sorry to disillusion you but paper is a drug

home?
better slow down

it's almost unbearable
i miss the trees
they'll be back

there didn't used to be t-shirts
or us
or anything

A Hard Line to Follow

yeah it hurt
but now we know we can do it
break our teeth on the songs the stones write with our bones

so the upshot of it all is a fountain of time
a light world to lift
a heavy rock to drop

dark art
just say the word & the subject drifts into the biblical sense of humour
drivers can open their eyes now

what a card
what a car
take it easy
we go far

DANCES

MARKING TIME

vincent was just trying to be a victorian landscape painter
late afternoon sun between cloud & gulf

i want that green
water's colour

city or not
close stones

surface all wet
magnified

air & eye
silence

light stops here
i've always wanted that green

one last drop of flor de caña black label 5 year old embottled rum
home i'm on the right track

all systems go
to bed

did anyone survive the election?
(silence)

as usual
b.c. knows something canada doesn't

each world a town
i think i'll catch the next road out

as soon as i see what this line says
dopes test best on the buddy system

portraits written
a dollar a minute

no-one can put you through like someone else
the time is now after you heard all this before but were you listening?

this is not what i want to think this is what i think
if i defend you from the editor will you defend me from myself?

a day spins around something done to it
the dentist a bath the soup a job the work a talk the kiss a book the twist

is that the same cigarette?
i thought we all left

no this is what i want to think
what i think is unthinkable

a life spins around the dance floor
a baby is born in alberta

lonely?
whistle read eat draw orgasm listen watch trip drink groom count rest wish

on the tape i edited out all the silences between ends of poems &
    beginnings of applause to see if i could write the audience
it didn't work

is there a question?
ask that & you'll never even want to

i asked you to cut my hair
you wouldn't

your glasses get stronger
your eyes larger

each time i see you these 30 years
we seized

we made a rule
make exceptions

potter throws herself around the earth
dish & bottle

poet folds himself into a corner
song & dance

it used to be 9 in the morning
but not any more

no my dear
don't have another beer

this writing is impaired
not inspired

repaired
not required

declared
not desired

i'll just adjust my bag strap
while the plastic's warm

refried
not free ride

writing is publishing
advertising is the kind of instruction you can't understand until too late

poetry is a martial art
i smoke about smoking

great lines ink alike
great feet stink alike

oh dear i've gone & figured us out
there goes the feeling i know you again

i had a bath
my gloves are in your bag

the pen found its own pocket
it was tv from 1000 years ago

i'd redecorate
but i did it right the 1st time

"jim byrnes is better than he was 10 years ago
more into it"

enacting the songs in it
is no act

no need to capitalize on your affinities
the furnace made it rain not me i explain to the cat

not applicable
anything you say

eat vitamins
bag sex

lose a watch
gain a wrist

this winter has been brought to you by last summer
have a strong week

A Bar Without Brakes

did i ever say i was scared
the last page of notebook 8124 add ink & stir
i'm scared
make my way
i said i was scared

●

on a good jukebox i'm every era i ever lived
now is the time for all good marxians to come to the aid of the marxists
cries from the video game behind me swamp
"o death what can i do"
you can always listen to the speakers

●

another tea to wash the jammed donut down
rest stop on the big nite out
totter home from all hours
bringing of old dreams up to day
roof of mouth tissue controls line endings
handwriting seems like me
first bus wrong direction
writing as habit amplified can cause age
SPEIACL
a spell
the power of a balance in the life
has pulled us through every raining day here
so fall this far

•

i feel like if i stopped to read the world
by the old light of this fool moon
filling that snappy black printjob of a sky

i'd crash in a flash
i'd explode in the road
i'd shatter in my tracks

i'd catch the cold clear fact
the truth lies
it's the wrong size

MY, TORONTO

beyond jupiter
security is light
before liberty
stupidity is might

waltzing the dog
wait up for my legs
it's not fair
you got two pair

contact me
-deum high
streetcar approaches
the first giggle of the toilet rushes by

famous fast words:
"where you goin?"
"none of your business
be here when i get back"

smiles meet
over a hot cup of
long odds
evening out to cabbagetown

doors closing on mortgages
i had to go back to calgary to type this out
"beginning of another perfect week?"
"well sort of"

god died for a couple days there
"mind the gap"
c.b.c. strikes out
country western is all my radio wears

the poor that be
the bees that pour
honey
gold as a loony on the streetcar track

the last of the winter ice used up sliding into town
"in t.o. everyone plays the game
in n.y.c. everyone cheats"
in montréal it's not a game

so finally
gorbachev says to the ukrainians:
"what do you want?"
"edmonton winnipeg poland"

("overly libidinous presence
tyrannizing 'psychic' space
unauthorized spring tour
emphatic mobility")

so i'm stumping the country for dave barrett
next conceptual leader of the n.d.p.
of course davey doesn't speak french
that's ok he speaks canadian

some of my best-dressed ancestors
been circling this home-made three-story brick city
since it was called "york"
of course i'm interested in anything you have to say about leaving

at the rex when the musicians finish a set
there's no need for recorded music
we know how to make a city go
all us keepers & weepers

the mirror's call
for the miracle
all you need is two bowls a house & a fridge
me & my emergency

but i don't know where the poetholders go
noisy cameras at pottery readings
not only focal place shutters but also auto advance
lucky we're not in combat these days

"i didn't expect that"
you said to that time in the sun
we looked away from what we were saying
& saw each other

cripes
words are supposed to float
the film on the walls is skin
we are the living proof of always

all saturday afternoon chasing winter north through our empty pockets
the few smokers left break out of the bus to sudbury
stretch into the wind
& fill it up

B U N D L E

The First Squirrel of Spring Thinks in Seeds

words planted in all these prairie cities
the route between
the roots of a hardy weed
with puzzling flowers
children pick

S'oon

the calendar is inaccurate here
you crop up every day
o mother of neighbourhoods

Identity Floss

play to the table
sing through your food

see to a sea
be to a beach

say it again say it again
golf

the rcmp station has the facilities to collect urine
yellow fire hydrant

hair do what hair does
part of the time

what have tractor caps & baseball caps got in common?
noodle soup

a beer under the game here
a coffee around the mural there

laughter in shatters
how so

Feed Me some Leads, Dad

a line takes off
a line closes

from now on it's now
no long time ago

is this seat free?
i'm afraid so

twice as long as i've been away from the new era in 14 years
where in the road does the road go

roll
fold

When My Beige Bic Turns to Pink Again

the bus driver thinks there's too many of us
so do we
decreasingly

the windows are clean to the north
i'm looking through a fine brown inscape
blown centre-lane mud painted on to the south

i'm just a guy who can't say yes
sit up straight & stare

wrong way right way
rub until rare

well done
when we dare

2002

you have every right to get that cross with me
there i go reading you your rights again

we didn't slow down to work fast enough
at this rate we'll pass that intractability sitting up ahead on a
    flatdeck by about 2002 when the kids are 12 21 29 39 41 always
    adding up to more than us

toss in a few foothills hear & their
makes for extra hectarage

i keep watching for that horse & cowboy i saw for a second out a train
    window nearby when i was 5
this spring i'll look that hard

be as sharp as a whitefish bone
the biggest skies get the best blues

in wainwright the bus stopped at a gas station so us guys squeezed
    the windows clean
i see

look
leaf

Edmonton Poems Is

finding the walking speed
very obvious
almost nil
keep to right on campus

i lost the house
the moon had moved to the back yard
the snow on the front lawn was all gone

personality a theory
my vision as blurred as the pen is sharp

spider trails light

Newt's Fly

the project is fusion
but not the way we thought

"there's gonna be a lotta lasers on the used art mart"
says the chemist at the next table

"the facts brook no distortion"
a chinese student asks me to explain

the intent is love
at room temperature

Stand Up Squirrel

& be seen
unbundle

as wide awake
as our very own star

see the mountains?
well so they are

in the sage
gaze

•

Budget Leak

the street of every
winnipig

saskartoon
edmontrap

calgory
regoona

the warrior flaunts
red wounds

face on
bayday

fear canada
can't control

one bloody
soul

Wild Rice

my longjohns are my sheets
exits

we don't have to talk
you said

insect
out

almost forgot my teeth
already i don't think i'm wearing new shoes

look at between us
we have just begun to listen

i missed what i wasn't saying
i was talking

exist
ants

Mooseburgers

i played with a fool breeze as i walked to the river
but that didn't cool me
i sat down like a jewel in a hand of empty grass
& shone upon the dying water

cigarette butt doesn't flow
floats & spins
where it was flicked
there it goes

"violation violation" quack the parking meters
space minus cash a crime
all those bridges frozen to broken promises
wrong premises

seen from history time is pain
seen from time history is panic

Bannock

safe at home
no-one
will ever know

open the door one morning
where in the world
did the earth go

robin
magpie
redwing blackbird

ate it
cold
flew away

laid it someplace new
& old

Reflex

reflect upon the picture
which in itself is a reflection upon a reflection
if not reflection on reflection

not counting the glass because in this case there isn't any
or the idea for the same reason

alone in the room
still water

your toes are wiggling your tongue
what you mean is blinking your eyes

reflected on the page
you reflect upon the page

sleep on it
reflection itself
as your self

Traces

bulletin
no it's the truth

a nest of copied leach pottery standardware gp bowls
general purpose
new stoneware in the tradition of
jeepers
tradition
the same body, shape, glazing and firing i have to go back 30 years to
  st ives cornwall to first see

all this time
surfacing in saskatchewan

it's not the wanting
that gets it right

a trace of paper
but not a trace of tail

Woodlot

there used to be a light here
moth waits by hole in ceiling with wires sticking out

frogs & crickets argue over who's who
dog gnaws skin off deer stick

people froze stiff
looking up into mountains of light

where there used to be night
the whole sky catches

like mind sees itself at speed
now that's fielding

or driving into falling
sunballs lost in birch, aspen, poplar, jackpine, white spruce, larch,
     groves, grandstands

planet spins
in the wind

or at table
venison from the bottle

coyote howl
well water

kids sleeping off ghost stories
trees about to be planted

somebody farts at a shooting star
goes back indoors speechless

dog
gone

Bin

i stumble unto grips with how the land is not flat where it matters
underfoot

pennies fall here from everywhere
& as soon as no-one's looking roll to the left along the webbed roads

i should have known
having slept over the rear axle

slab by slab to regina illegible
the bus from it matters too much

disorder is what it takes
every spring how it is grows back a little steeper

& the heavy machinery is out there plowing it under
under orders from some dust devil down at the flat white bank of nowhere

northern virgin forests still getting bulldozed
but like stones in a field we spot each other & know where

Gravel

the beavers are saved
their pelts don't fetch what it costs the subsistence farmers to catch them
so it's up to ranchers & fastfarmers to skin the overpopulating critters
  with dynamite
for flooding the money

the willows are blushing
the dry grass rustles its dust
at what the first bee said to the first mosquito
"direct drive is a really high gear"

the forest sinks into the shadow of the horizon
handwriter enters trance ten weeks ago
everybody knows best
just asking

wades with the sauna buckets into the lake without breaking the ice
  thinking
"well if i'm not going to be spending 20 billion on war toys i suppose
  i can afford to go home"

Postcard

i smiled over to your invitation
to join you in conversation

over coffee at your table
in the shade of the cafe

the afternoon after the day
i got to the end of the line

"sorry"
spilling a little i said

"i'm sitting outside
writing you"

in the farmyard of bumpy memory
the dog's softball & the bucktooth skull

come to a different standstill
each time the kids have to be told the same old thing

Talk Talking

car with right rear wheel up on the sidewalk taking a park
dog took keys out of the trunk lock & put them on the doorstep

is our new embassy on pennsylvania ave part of the u.s. go't
like it looks

or a de't store
i sprinkle salt on a glass of beer when i want columns

& then there's the human race
we lie down where we can see to close our eyes

the present is on a slope
around the hill

we can almost reach
our hands touch

hands
we imagine

D I P

thong?

where the day
out
night int
o

Head Winds

i discovered
immediately after taking the back to normal
great shit of the late '80s
30 mistakes in the news story i was reading

a phantom of a man behind a dusty window
cuts or lips or leaves all over his skin
standing looking at the moment before ambition
you saw him too

sinews singing i'm
15 minutes late already
that won't last long

"i'm sure glad you're coming
bro'
because i don't have any money"

Lost Illusions

the household that doesn't twist the phone cord gets the familiar teller

the more times you push the button for the walk sign
the longer it seems
the fewer
the longer it is

he who can wind the clock without counting will remember that the
   hollow handle of the disposable razor is filled with water

people with good posture won't sit in front of you at the movies if
   you're watching the screen with binoculars

"chickens have absolutely no brain
you cut their head off & they run around
because they're confused
they don't know what's happened
because they have no brain
the only reason they die
is they bleed to death"

Caution: Automatic Poem

we could look into each other forever
perhaps we will someday

i deserve another something or other
"grit your fingers"

89
handwrites in one line

fart & toothpaste
the smell of government art

success is for suckers
the little fish you catch for bait

gun control vs pro life
a yankee standoff

canadian guys in conversation clutching their beer bottles
like it's the smile in their voice

Be Peaceful

can't hear
or did i forget to listen

did you win? "no
but the other team did"

buried even
home is in the way

i remember when i was in love
i liked everyone else but i didn't have to

"guns are always loaded"
hands off tibet

maybe it's just me
maybe i'm counting on it

sure is easy to read
alone

NIDLIGHT MUNCH

simulation for the nation
by
toronto in july

if only what it is
were also what it's not
not only what it sold
but also what it bought

a line of wine
a joke of bread
and
chew

"the minute he stepped in the house
my whole body was alert"

walk home
& you'll stay home longer

"lords, i protest my soul is full of woe
that blood should sprinkle me to make me grow"

"cup your smoke under your palm
just so & everybody'll know
you've been to reform school"

"you a republican
a democrat
or a calm eye?"

too weak is too bleak again
to wank is to blank again
to wink is to blink again

growing up on stage
you couldn't do better myself
thank electricity for heaven

what do you call this season?
"shorts"

i can tell
can't you tell?
a racist commercial when we see one

rattling
passing
for laughter

push
town
like being an undimensional fly in a sci-fi wallet

i even had the radio on
i even changed the station
i even turned it off

can't listen to musicians
not seeing through frank zappa

cat
on
a
hot
squirrelskin
leash

cubist
rock
a
century
of
guitar
&
bottle

born that
worn this
way

meanwhile
back at the afterlife
goes on

i'm on the can
leave a message
after the splash

clever nuts
all shell
smashed in canada

heavy sweating
glueing what comes factually

GRAMPS

the west is warm & wet
best
in august

Don't Touch that Whiteout

man retching in the alley drowns out radio news
i rush in the house & apply late july koto records
his gut relaxes
hold it
go upstairs & check out alley raving
or let it pass
only a fiction in the telling

i got a job
wait'll they get the bill

Candle

it's the wax that burns
the candle

as it comes
take it

my eyes become accustomed
you are

lovely
i have lit a candle

Cassandra, Born 5:07 A.M.

welcome
to our well

a world
kneel

drink
mind

breathe
that's the spirit

dream
rising

dance
raining

all you
are here

HISSES

welcome
to our well

a world
kneel

drink
mind

breathe
that's the spririt

dream
rising

dance
raining

all here
you are

my landlord caught me pretending i never slept
i'd look balefully at him when we'd meet in the courtyard

he understood that it's all this writing is how it goes
that i don't have money this era & set the rent accordingly

japanese expects canadian poetry
eventually

i keep the cats still looking good
& love to hold the gate open for everyone

trim the ivy
tie the fence to it

re-position the bin in front of the gap each week
troop the family feast to the restaurant through the kitchen betimes

the porch light's on for you
the alley goes right on by all night

smelts are running
that line of gulls out there on a line of floats

monday is my day off from needing my own reading
me & a pastrami sandwich & high tide at kits beach crumbling

sun so far away
music so near

no fear
not this old bird on the sand with a fish-long stick in her beak

comes on strong to another gull & gets him to want it
a round of yelling

money's a copy of what you haven't got
the more money the more you haven't got

live blue currencies rippling in the sunset
she's at it again

i remember now
i was dying

it was very physical
wearing down on the inside

a great comfort seeing all those people on the wall being paid to act
3 blossoms on the hydrangea this summer & the bamboo & the ferns & the
  holly berries swirl around them

vacuumed today
thought i'd lost all that hair

nothing like a slow bath to loosen up the music on the radio
a fly's like a baby crying

beginning of september & everyone's drifting back by themselves
plain colours on plain sails set to catch the slightest idea

whispers of garbage trucks 2 nights away
so quiet with the furnace off

it's just
muscular

a
rib cage

twitch
you wouldn't be interested

faulty summer
recall memory

i'd buy new jeans
but i can't find any with the right knee out

labour'd
eh

rake the sand on the desk
file the piles

if this is in print i didn't write it
"what force might gain, force must maintain"
the world is only what there was time for
awake is a sexually transmitted disease, see
some days you just gotta live well & will you sing or will you whistle?
the native indian guy who got the paper outa the paperbox & extracted
   the tv guide for himself came back & gave the rest of the paper which
   he'd left on top of the box to 2 young asian women there at the bus
   stop & they took it & then he came back again to see if they wanted
   tv guides too & they didn't catch his english but they kept the
   paper for sure & some of us talked about it & whitey's writing it up
can't stop now, i lost the lid of the pen on the bus, applaud when
   you've heard enough
watch out for poems doing what they're saying
i see that neutrinos are in the news again, it seems that space
   comes to them
o they'll get some fat jack nicholson of the future to play noriega
"mall, hell, it's just an endless stream of people going back & forth"
the headlines the day after nelson mandela's release from prison went
   from ARMED STRUGGLE GOES ON to
   COMMITTED TO PEACE to STEP UP THE
   FIGHT to FREEDOM FOR ALL or was it free for all
at the "speed of silence"

don't you just hate it when:

someone in vancouver turns out prepared for the february blizzard?

you can't get a simple compact-cassette tape recorder with a *line out?*

some days you don't even think about the one you love?

the coin that popped outa your pocket was a dollar & he sez "thankyou,
   sir" quotes & all & you know you're not as poor as you thought?

the words are inside the rimes?

it turns out that the thing you've been fighting for all your life turns
   out to be a chance to disarm the gunman before he turns out any more
   damage?

your self turns into walking along at about the same speed as my self?

the book you're eating is better than the book you're reading?

you had to be there & you were & you remember what you learned & you
   wake up & somebody's made you into a snowman & it's a lovely
   sunny day?

you don't wait for at least an hour before going to bed after seeing
   bad thinking?

sun ra sez it's fantastic swing but it's out there at the same time?

trolley sez the local is lo cal?

you can get custom crafted hours in about a glass?

the skin smiles?

ok?
yeah go ahead
i mean back up!

why don't they make bran muffins in the shape of turds
shit
that's the idea

how about let's not think of anything we didn't read first
where does that leave us?
"you made me read you . . ."

they're talking about cyril colony on the national
which isn't
either

this rattler's just an old bicycle
powered by natural ass

there were little faces in all that writing on the page, words
as soon as we saw it, a language
all at once talking & singing to the imagination

venus de milo is also
everyone staring at the broken point of the pencil
lost in thought

then came reading writing & arithmetic
poetry the trick to read what can't be said
quick to say what can't be read

cite sight site, kneeling at the window
write right rite, in the eye of day
alight a light alight, at the ear of night

a world can turn on the page
a page can turn on the world

head off ego central at the face in the mirror
before there are no more free rivers & forests in bc
before the skies are totally fried
& the stink of extinction has shrivelled memory

temper on a
bit of a short
leash you see
i hurt

but this time this petal didn't fall off
just stripped a layer or two of chest muscle
shaking like mad back & forth
after the pedal hit that impossible curve

until all that's left of us is the balance
the world hangs in

fools rule

a day a year
an era a kalpa
a zero a one
an ocean a tear
a blossom an apple
a nipple a tongue

a sewage burning plant an airborne hepatitis
awakening up at the movies after a dry drunk
a barbara frum a pierre trudeau, agent provocateur
a sliding home a being born in reverse
a not reaching for my wallet once that night at the pub & so losing it
a roland kirk of all that wants to be said

rules fool

erasing the second two-thirds
of a previous reader's
light non-herbal marginal pencillings, tracks
in a hardcover library copy of willeford's new hope for the dead
but the first third of the book i left them in
having lived with trying to find the pattern to them
and failing
and not wanting to deal with them anymore

over a cox's orange pippin
after dinner
watching the fog thicken
in kitsilano

instructions in the dream to: boil the buckle
the brass buckle i bought at the blind owl more than twenty years ago?

under the bogey photo of who won
beside the dali desert of no when

". . . today — & tomorrow as well"

now for the requite i mean rewrite
boil the buckle
oh i get it now

from now on i want all my books published in pencil, ok?

makes the paper
easier
to recycle

the words better
to remember

the point harder to resist
that the poem is in your words now

eyes stung closed
balls kicked
nose batted
face muskegged
hands strapped & bitten
ass thrashed
teeth drilled
arm broken
foreskin snipped
knee line drived
eardrum scarred
wrist burned
ankles twisted
so far so good

good friday
the 13th

let's go sniff
the rich

they
know

not
how

offensive
their

i can't get no self-satisfaction
is

but they
smell nice

did you see that november tv commercial
when the woodward family lost control of their business
where the apostrophe-ess drops off the name

"are these the most important seconds today?" he thought
from his seat in the back of the bus
staring at the bag of rags someone just left in the aisle
& with an expert's look of disgust at the crowd elbowed her way out
as if it were hers & had a bomb in it
"no, it's mine" he thought of it "no, it's not"
"it's just that
it's true that
it's not true"

leaves we call them
leaving us behind

write now
eco's novel sells 8 million
read then
vancouver sun calls it unreadable
now write
radio goes on
then read
one song
write then
too long
read now
then write
the attention span of a slug
now read

if you lost a purple lighter at my last reading
it ran out on me too

it's my home
town but anglais canada's still arguing about abstract art

i bet lithuania & all those other countries revvin' up for democracy
  on their own getta lotta press in québec
french really wants all its law back

the b.c. forests industry explains that all the trees it didn't replant
  in the past century will be right back
after the break

at which point puss positive gags up a 3 inch blade of grass
slime shiny

no-one can give away the terrible & beautiful responsibility for
  life & death
the dot on the eye of our individuality

we we we
all the way home

i suppose the cat at the airplane window meows & scratches the glass
funny how we say what we mean but suddenly that's not what it's made
   of anymore

politics as an intercontinental fear of love
we give you debt, you give us the willies

maybe canada's just not got the courage to be a nation
maybe the conservatives are right & we should apply for homeland status
   at the u.n.

let's take back roads to far towns coast to coast to coast
wanna go? or you wanna stand there pissin' on your runners

this is a write-up
i need a match for the nite half of the j of the day

7 months today without tobacco, a long wave
small deal, big lead

silk scarfs flutter from the gates we are for each other
all the heart involved lives on

days & tasks
ours, all our hours at once, a day
belong to history

intricate hands, simple butts, soft
the flesh of poetry between languages, the task
my days & tasks belong to history

hisssssss treeeeeee

i don't know i'm here writing
i think i'm out in the city thinking this up
this glance of words
this living i make
when of course it's the chance
the body
thinking me up

response ability
or is it talent

now if only my teeth can last the millenium
grinding away at the same old stones

democracy's the government that comes when it's called
grows up & old all over again like anybody & goes when it's told

another stupid man smashing the masks a quarter century ago after reading at
   last exit to brooklyn & genet & cocteau & miller & poe
& that scene made it into the movie

from shut up & listen to
think fast: don't move

"his prosodic and phonic art is so great
that to some ears his humanity barely rescues it from preciosity"

beautiful bones
last & last

syllables adrift
the beach of speech

a sift of dry sand
thin inch

a face on the under
standing in us

me "ss universe tied up at pier b.c."
you "it was bound to happen sooner or later"

desire
memory on fire

passion
eating dream

surprise
or our lives will have nothing to do with us